EYE ON THE SKY

WHEN HAIL HITS

Gareth Stevens PUBLISHING

BY CHRISTINE HONDERS

Please visit our website, www.garethstevens.com. For a free color catalog of all our high-quality books, call toll free 1-800-542-2595 or fax 1-877-542-2596.

Library of Congress Cataloging-in-Publication Data

Honders, Christine.
When hail hits / by Christine Honders.
p. cm. — (Eye on the sky)
Includes index.
ISBN 978-1-4824-2884-1 (pbk.)
ISBN 978-1-4824-2885-8 (6 pack)
ISBN 978-1-4824-2886-5 (library binding)
1. Hail — Juvenile literature. I. Honders, Christine. II. Title.
QC929.H15 H65 2016
551.57'87—d23

Published in 2016 by
Gareth Stevens Publishing
111 East 14th Street, Suite 349
New York, NY 10003

Designer: Laura Bowen
Editor: Kristen Rajczak

Photo credits: Cover, p. 1 Virginia Star/Moment Open/Getty Images; cover, pp. 1–32 (series art) Nik Merkulov/Shutterstock.com; p. 5 (main) © iStockphoto.com/shimmo; p. 5 (inset) Ryszard Stelmachowicz/Shutterstock.com; p. 7 Patrick Hamilton/Stringer/AFP/Getty Images; p. 9 Minerva Studio/Shutterstock.com; p. 11 Lee Yiu Tung/Shutterstock.com; p. 12 Brian0918/Wikimedia Commons; p. 13 (background) Glg/Wikimedia Commons; p. 14 Nelson Almeida/AFP/Getty Images; p. 15 (satellite image) NOAA/Getty Images News/Getty Images; p. 15 (cars) Mauricio Duenas/AFP/Getty Images; p. 16 (glass) Win Henderson/Wikimedia Commons; p. 16 (siding) Hyoung Chang/Denver Post/Getty Images; p. 17 (main) Steve Nehf/Denver Post/Getty Images; p. 17 (inset) John Preito/Denver Post/Getty Images; p. 19 Annie Griffiths Belt/National Geographic/Getty Images; p. 21 PerseoMedusa/Shutterstock.com; p. 23 (background) Karen Hedley/Wikimedia Commons; p. 23 (radar dome) Education Images/Universal Images Group/Getty Images; p. 25 (golf balls) Jack Dagley Photography/Shutterstock.com; p. 25 (peas) © iStockphoto.com/Westhoff; p. 26 Ssnowball/Shutterstock.com; p. 27 (main) Karl Gehring/Denver Post/Getty Images; p. 27 (inset) Jim Edds/Science Source/Getty Images; p. 28 Photo Researchers/Science Source/Getty Images; p. 29 (top left) deepspacedave/Shutterstock.com; p. 29 (top right) NWS Aberdeen, SD/Wikimedia Commons; p. 29 (bottom left) ERZ/Wikimedia Commons; p. 29 (bottom right) National Severe Storms Laboratory Collection/Wikimedia Commons.

Printed in the United States of America

CPSIA compliance information: Batch #CS15GS: For further information contact Gareth Stevens, New York, New York at 1-800-542-2595.

CONTENTS

Words in the glossary appear in **bold** type the first time they are used in the text.

ICE FROM THE SKY

You're outside on a bright summer day. Dark clouds start to swirl around in the sky, and thunder begins to rumble. There's a storm coming! The rain falls all around as you run for cover. Summer thunderstorms happen all the time, so you're not surprised.

What happens next? Small balls of ice fall to the ground. How can ice fall from the sky in the middle of summertime? These ice balls are called hail, and they can fall any time of the year. This book will explain where hail comes from and what happens during and after a hailstorm.

HAIL ALLEY

Hailstorms are most common during the summer months in mild climates. The area where Nebraska, Colorado, and Wyoming meet is known as "Hail Alley," where hail falls around 7 to 9 days each year, more than anywhere else in the United States. China, Russia, India, and northern Italy also have severe hailstorms.

Hailstorms can happen any time of year, all over the world, and with hailstones of many different shapes and sizes.

EXPENSIVE WEATHER

There are lots of dangers in a severe thunderstorm, like lightning or **tornadoes**. Although hail doesn't usually cause injury to people, it can destroy homes, businesses, and crops. Even hail the size of a pea can destroy a farmer's entire field by ripping the plants to shreds. Large hailstones can break windows, **damage** rooftops, and dent automobiles.

In the United States, hail causes almost $1 billion in damage every year. Hail was the major cause of damage during one of the most severe storms in recent history. It occurred in April 2003, lasted 3 days, and swept over 10 states. The storm caused $1.6 billion in damage!

SOCCER BALL–SIZED HAIL!

The largest hailstone ever measured in the United States fell in Vivian, South Dakota, on June 23, 2010. It was 8 inches (20 cm) wide with a **circumference** of almost 19 inches (48 cm). It was as big as a soccer ball! Hailstones this big sometimes contain stuff like leaves, stones, and even bugs.

Hailstones as big as tennis balls damaged many cars and homes in Australia during a storm in November 2014.

WHAT IS HAIL?

Hail is a type of precipitation, which is water that falls to Earth in the form of rain, ice, or snow. Hailstones are lumps of ice that fall from thunderstorm clouds. They're sometimes round with a rough surface and are usually between 0.2 and 6 inches (0.5 and 15 cm) in **diameter**. Most hail is about the size of a pea.

Small hail is created during strong thunderstorms. Lucky for us, hailstorms don't last very long and don't cover large areas. Very strong thunderstorms, called supercell thunderstorms, can make hailstones ranging from the size of a quarter to the size of a volleyball!

WHERE DOESN'T HAIL FALL?

Warm climates in places like Florida have many thunderstorms every year, but almost never have hail. That's because in these climates, the hail has to fall through a warm layer of air at the bottom of a thunderstorm, which melts the hailstones before they reach the ground.

Supercell thunderstorms are very strong thunderstorms that last longer than ordinary thunderstorms. They can make tornadoes with winds up to 200 miles (322 km) per hour!

WHERE DOES HAIL COME FROM?

To understand how hail is made, we need to understand what happens inside a storm cloud.

There's water in the air we breathe, but we can't see it because it's in the form of water vapor. During warm weather, the sun heats the air near the ground. As it heats up, it rises, and as it rises, the air cools down. Cool air can't hold as much water vapor as warm air, so the vapor condenses, meaning it turns from vapor into water droplets. These droplets collect on tiny pieces of dust. When millions and millions of these droplets get together, they form clouds.

STORMY WEATHER

The white, puffy clouds we see are cumulus clouds. If a cumulus cloud rises into the cooler air, it turns into a cumulonimbus cloud. As cumulonimbus clouds rise, they start to look dark and grey—they're thunderclouds! The word "cumulonimbus" comes from two Latin words: *cumulus*, which means "**accumulated**," and *nimbus*, which means "rain."

Cumulonimbus clouds are taller than other clouds and look like mushrooms. The base of the cloud is sometimes several miles wide!

INSIDE THE THUNDERHEAD

During a storm, strong winds blow upwards and downwards. These winds are called updrafts and downdrafts. Rain falls from the cumulonimbus clouds, also known as "thunderheads." The raindrops get caught in the updrafts and downdrafts, tossing them up and down.

layers inside a hailstone

Most thunderheads grow to **altitudes** of over 25,000 feet (7,620 m). The top of the thunderhead, where the air is the coldest, contains supercooled water. When an updraft pushes frozen raindrops, tiny ice crystals, and dust to the top of the thunderhead, they meet the supercooled water. The supercooled water freezes to them, making hailstones.

This diagram shows how hail forms inside a cloud.

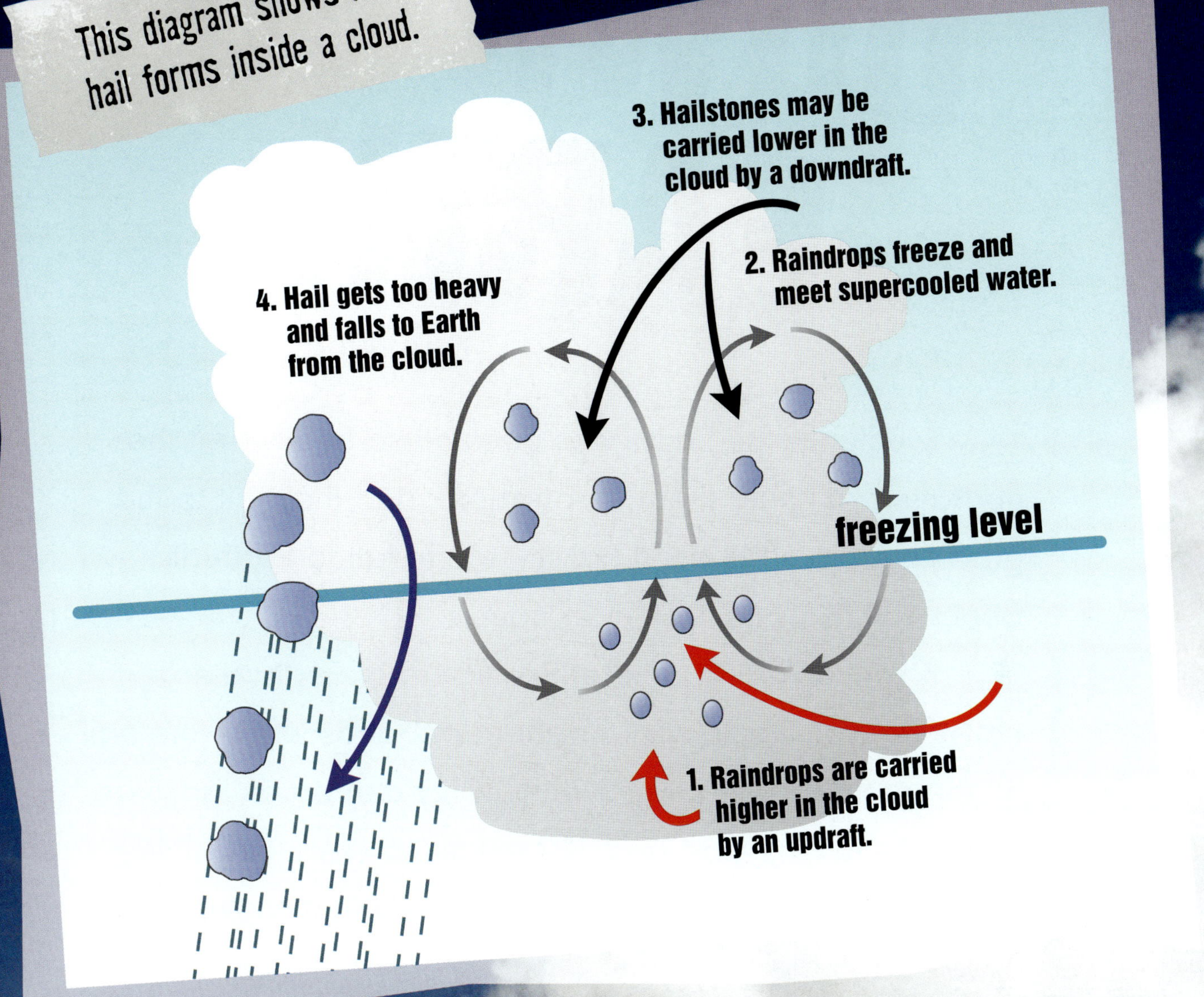

LAYER UP

The stronger the updraft, the more times the hailstone is lifted to the top of the cloud, making it bigger and bigger. If you cut open a hailstone, it has layers, like an onion. The more layers it has, the more times it's traveled up and down inside the thunderhead.

DOWN TO EARTH

Eventually the hailstones become so heavy that the updrafts can't hold them up anymore, and they fall to the ground. A baseball-sized hailstone can fall to Earth at about 100 miles (161 km) per hour.

If you looked at a **satellite** picture of Earth after a hailstorm, you would see a pattern of bands where the hail hit the ground called hail swaths. They can be as large as 10 miles (16 km) wide and 100 miles (161 km) long! Piles of hail in hail swaths have been so deep that snowplows have had to dig them out.

Storms that may produce hail can be seen using weather satellites.

FROZEN FACTS

Hail is only one type of frozen precipitation. Sleet is balls of ice smaller than hail that fall during the winter months. Snow is made when water vapor turns to ice. These don't commonly occur during a thunderstorm. Graupel (GRAU-puhl) is a small ice pellet that's made when supercooled water coats a snowflake.

THE HAIL IS FALLING!

Hail doesn't cause as much injury as other severe weather, but that doesn't mean you shouldn't take cover. Hail isn't usually very big, but it does lots of damage in a short time. It would feel like being hit by marbles falling from the sky!

The amount of damage hail causes depends on how big the hailstones are. Hailstones larger than about 2 inches (5 cm) can break roof tiles, dent cars, and break car windshields. Strong winds make it worse by blowing hailstones into the sides of houses. Hail causes the most damage to crops because even the smallest hailstones destroy growing fruits and vegetables.

Hailstorms like the one in 2013 aren't uncommon in Denver, Colorado.

DUMPING ON DENVER

In September 2013, a hailstorm pounded the city of Denver. The hailstones clogged storm drains, and, combined with rain, caused flooding in the streets. People were trapped in some places by piles of hail 5 feet (1.5 m) tall! Dump trucks and front loaders were brought in to dig them out.

RECORD-SETTING HAIL

One of the worst hailstorms in American history happened on March 29, 2012, in McAllen, Texas. Baseball-sized hail slammed the town, leaving almost 6 inches (15 cm) of hail on the ground! Another Texas storm on June 13, 2012, caused nearly $2 billion in damage.

Alberta, Canada, gets more hailstorms than anywhere else in Canada. If fact, parts of Alberta are called Canada's "Hail Alley." In August 2014, a violent storm dropped tennis ball-sized hail on Alberta. This storm wiped out a year's worth of a farmer's crops in just a few minutes.

INTERNATIONAL HAIL OF FAME

The deadliest hailstorm on record occurred in Moradabad, India, on April 30, 1888. Back then, there was no way to warn people about approaching storms, so many people were working in the fields when this storm hit. Orange-sized hailstones hammered the town, killing 230 people and thousands of farm animals.

Hail costs farmers millions and millions of dollars every year. Many farmers pay for crop insurance, which helps them recover some of the money lost during a hailstorm.

CAN HAIL BE STOPPED?

In the 14th century, people in Europe thought they could stop hail by firing cannons into the air. Some people, especially farmers, still believe that hail cannons prevent hail. Hail cannons use **combustible** gas and air to fire **shock waves** into a thundercloud to break up hail as it's forming. Most **meteorologists** don't believe they work.

Cloud seeding, which is a method of shooting chemicals into clouds to cause more rain, is believed by some scientists to prevent large hailstones. Not everyone agrees that it works, and some people think the chemicals that are used in cloud seeding are harmful.

THE GOLD MEDAL FOR WEATHER

China uses cloud seeding as a way to make rain for farmers, clear away air pollution, and to provide its large population with enough water. China also experiments with other kinds of weather control. In fact, during the Beijing Olympics in 2008, it used rockets to shoot rain clouds out of the sky!

Even though scientists don't believe in them, some farmers swear that hail cannons work. They're still used in Italian vineyards.

WEATHER PREDICTION

Most meteorologists agree the best way to prepare for a hailstorm is to become better at **predicting** them. Since the 1990s, weather forecasters have used **Doppler radar**, which shows how much precipitation is in a thundercloud and the direction the storm is moving.

Doppler radar can't tell exactly what kind of precipitation is in the cloud, so in 2012 the National Weather Service added an update to their radar called dual-polarized (dual-pol) technology. Dual-pol technology gives meteorologists a better look at the precipitation so that they can tell the difference between rain, hail, and snow. This helps the public make better decisions about their safety.

DUAL DIMENSIONAL

Dual-pol technology can tell the difference between rain and hail because it sees a two-dimensional image of the precipitation. "Two-dimensional" means you can tell how wide and tall something is from a picture, which is something Doppler radar couldn't do before.

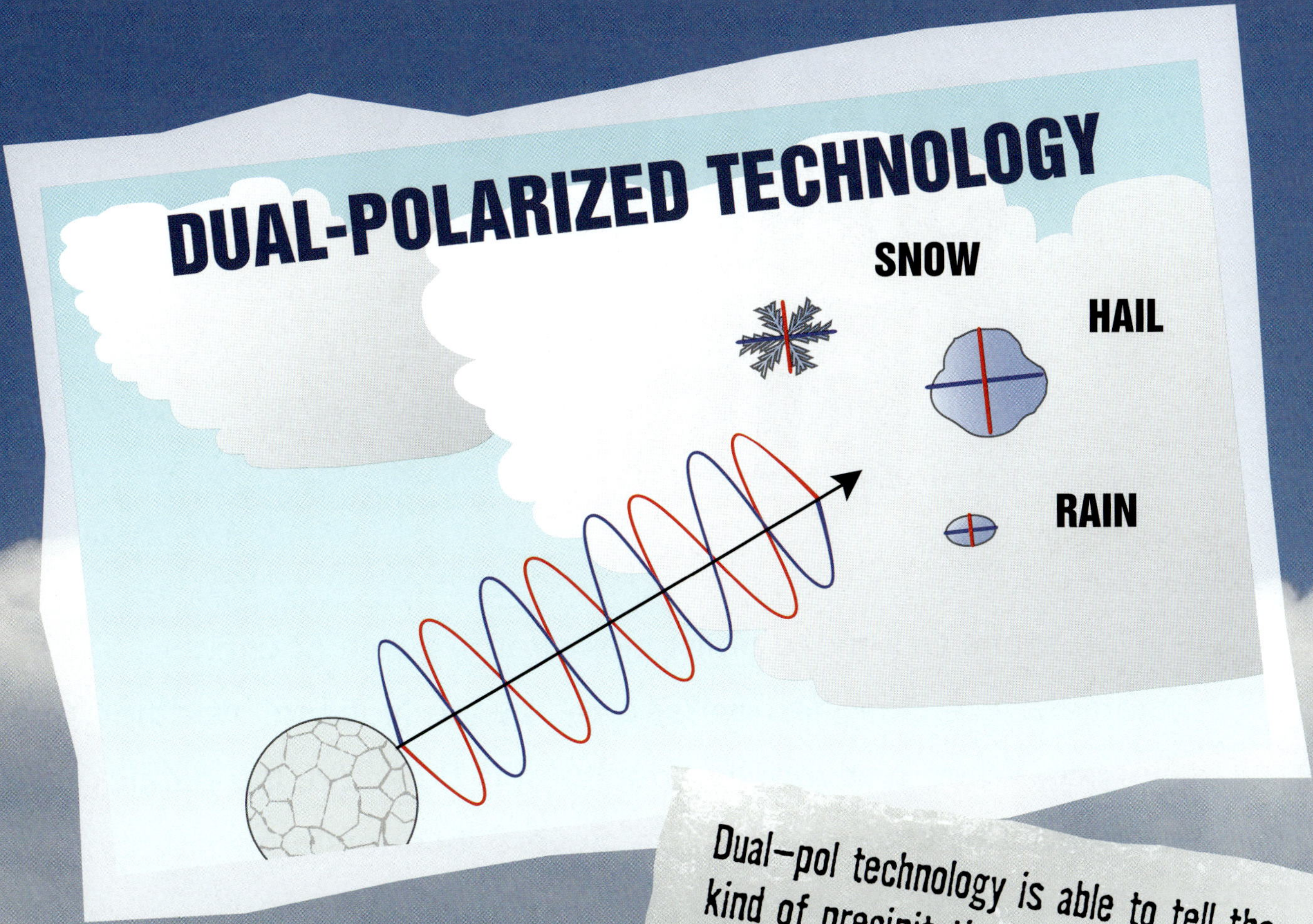

Dual–pol technology is able to tell the kind of precipitation that will fall during a storm based on its shape.

SAFETY FIRST

Storms that make hailstones over 3/4 inch (2 cm) in diameter are classified as "severe" by the National Weather Service. When a severe thunderstorm is detected, the public is notified so they can prepare. Severe thunderstorms not only make hail, but have winds over 58 miles (93 km) per hour.

If you're in an area where a severe thunderstorm has been spotted, you need to get to the nearest building as quickly as you can! You should go to an **interior** room on the ground floor and stay away from windows. Cars, boats, and open areas aren't places to be during a severe thunderstorm.

MORE HARD-HITTING WEATHER

Hail isn't the only thing we need to worry about during a severe storm. Tornadoes, flooding, and lightning can also cause a lot of damage. If the National Weather Service gives a severe storm warning in your town, don't ignore it! Take action quickly to keep yourself safe.

HAIL SIZES

pea	1/4 inch (0.6 cm)
marble	1/2 inch (1.3 cm)
mothball	1/2 inch (1.3 cm)
dime	3/4 inch (1.9 cm)
penny	3/4 inch (1.9 cm)
nickel	7/8 inch (2.2 cm)
quarter	1 inch (2.5 cm)
half-dollar	1 1/4 inches (3.2 cm)
walnut	1 1/2 inches (3.8 cm)
Ping-Pong ball	1 1/2 inches (3.8 cm)
golf ball	1 3/4 inches (4.4 cm)
hen's egg	2 inches (5 cm)
tennis ball	2 1/2 inches (6.4 cm)
baseball	2 3/4 inches (7 cm)
teacup	3 inches (7.6 cm)
grapefruit	4 inches (10 cm)
softball	4 1/2 inches (11.4 cm)

Hailstone sizes are compared to the size of everyday objects, making them easier to measure and record. The National Weather Service uses these terms.

LIFE IN HAIL ALLEY

If you live in a place like Hail Alley where more hail falls than any other place in the country, you might take action to protect yourself and your property. It's a good idea to keep an emergency kit handy with a few days worth of food, water, flashlights, and a battery-powered radio in case you lose power.

Some homes have roofs made of tough materials, like slate or rubber, to protect against the cracking and damage that hail causes. Hail protection netting is available to farmers who want to keep their crops from being torn up by hail.

Colorado is in the top 10 of US states every year for hailstorm damage. A 3-day storm with hail in May 2014 cost the state $109.3 million in damage!

AIRBAGS ON THE OUTSIDE

About 250,000 cars are damaged by hail in the United States every year. One company decided to make an airbag for the outside of the car! The driver enables the airbag from their cell phone, and the airbag fills with air in less than 5 minutes. It supposedly protects cars against softball-sized hail.

WHEN HAIL HITS!

The next time you're in a hailstorm, wait until it's over and collect the hailstones. How big are they? Are they round or lumpy? If you cut them open, how many layers do you see? You can get an idea of how strong a storm was just by looking at its hailstones.

If you're outside on a sunny summer day and see thunderclouds forming in the sky, be aware. It's important to remember that a thunderstorm can turn dangerous very quickly, and hail isn't something to be taken lightly. Now you know what to do when hail hits!

This hailstone spent a lot of time in the thunderhead and probably collided with other hailstones when it fell.

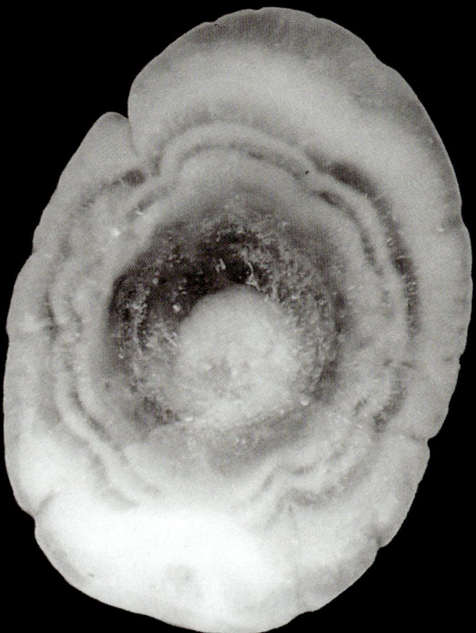

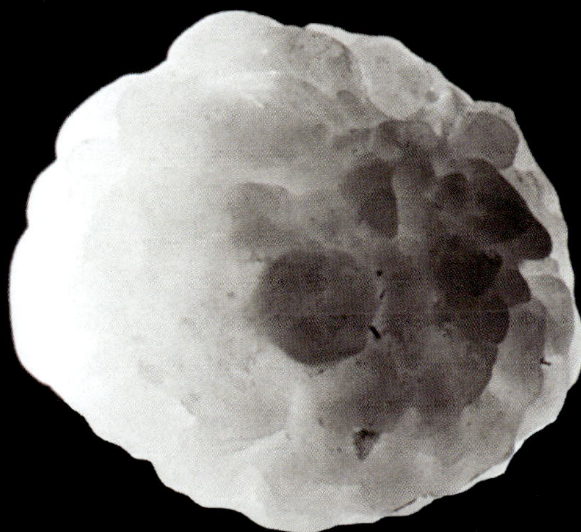

THE SHAPE OF HAIL

When most people think of hail, they think of smooth, round balls of ice. But during its trip from the sky to Earth, it picks up objects like dirt, twigs, leaves, and even other hailstones. This gives many hailstones, usually the larger ones, all kinds of interesting shapes.

GLOSSARY

accumulate: to increase little by little over time

altitude: the height above sea level

circumference: the length around the widest part of a ball

combustible: able to be burned easily

damage: harm. Also, to cause harm.

diameter: the distance from one side of a round object to another through its center

Doppler radar: a machine that uses radio waves to locate and identify objects and also measures the speed and direction objects are moving

interior: inside

meteorologist: someone who studies weather, climate, and the atmosphere

predict: to guess what will happen in the future based on facts or knowledge

satellite: an object that circles Earth in order to collect and send information or aid in communication

shock wave: a sharp change of pressure traveling in the air caused by an explosion

tornado: a funnel-shaped cloud that touches the ground and is accompanied by strong winds that can cause damage

FOR MORE INFORMATION

BOOKS

Kostigen, Thomas. *Extreme Weather: Surviving Tornadoes, Sandstorms, Hailstorms, Blizzards, Hurricanes, and More!* Washington, DC: National Geographic Children's Books, 2014.

Snedeker, Joe. *The Everything Kids' Weather Book: From Tornadoes to Snowstorms, Puzzles, Games, and Facts That Make Weather for Kids Fun!* Avon, MA: Adams Media, 2012.

WEBSITES

Amazing Hail Storm
www.sciencekids.co.nz/videos/weather/hailstorm.html
See just how destructive hail can be and watch a video of hail in action.

Weather Wiz Kids
www.weatherwizkids.com/
Find out more fascinating facts about hail and other kinds of severe weather.

Publisher's note to educators and parents: Our editors have carefully reviewed these websites to ensure that they are suitable for students. Many websites change frequently, however, and we cannot guarantee that a site's future contents will continue to meet our high standards of quality and educational value. Be advised that students should be closely supervised whenever they access the Internet.

INDEX